MW00947179

Map Legend

Borders

Country border
National Park border
Military/restricted area
Fence
Gate

Roads & Paths

Surfaced roads
Dirt roads & tracks
Walking trails
Restricted/guided trails
Obligatory walking direction

Natural Terrain

Lakes, ponds
Wood
Glacier
Cliffs
Viewpoint
Cave entrance

Man-made Features

Power line
Railroad
Pipeline

Quarry
Monument, tourist attraction
Downhill skiing routes & lifts

Amenities

 Rangers post
 Police station; border control
Tourist information
Hotel, hostel
Guest house; alpine hut
Staffed/Commercial campsite
Closed campsite
Hospital
Post office
Playground

Transportation & Transport Amenities

Car parking
Bus station/hub
Bus stop
Ferry & cruise ship routes
Airport

Food

Cafe, restaurant, bakery
Grocery store; supermarket

All Elevations are in Meters
Mercator Projection SAD 69

Sergio Mazitto Tourist Topo Maps

Available from
Amazon.com and other retailers

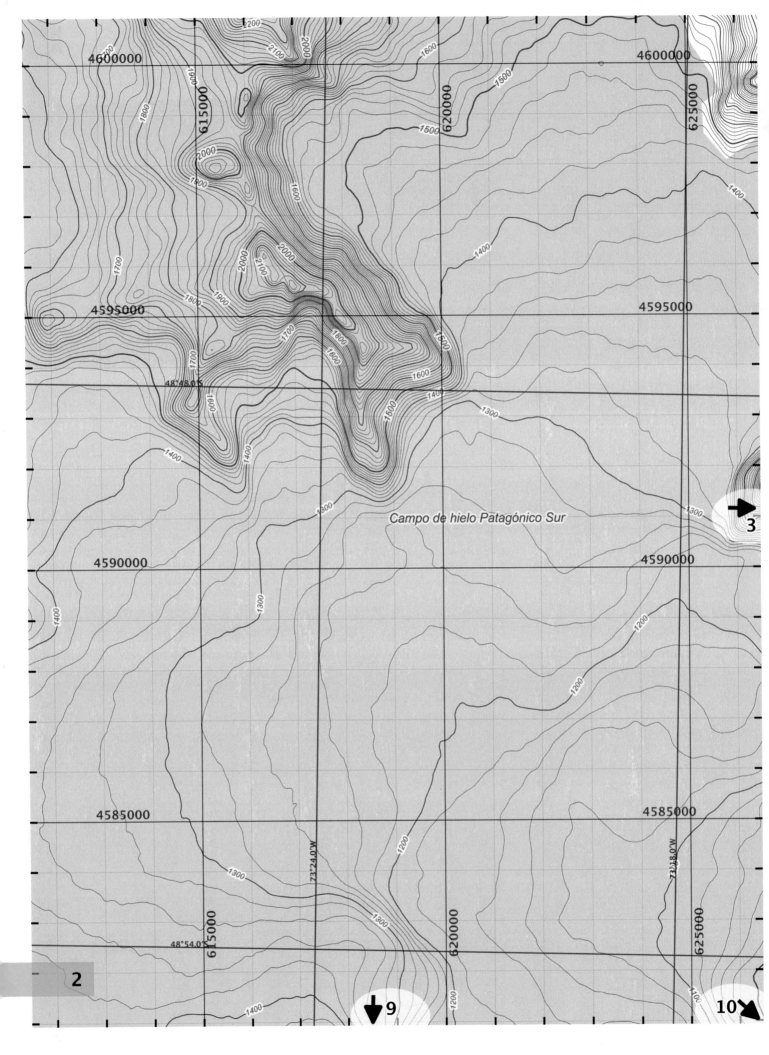

Campo de hielo Patagónico Sur

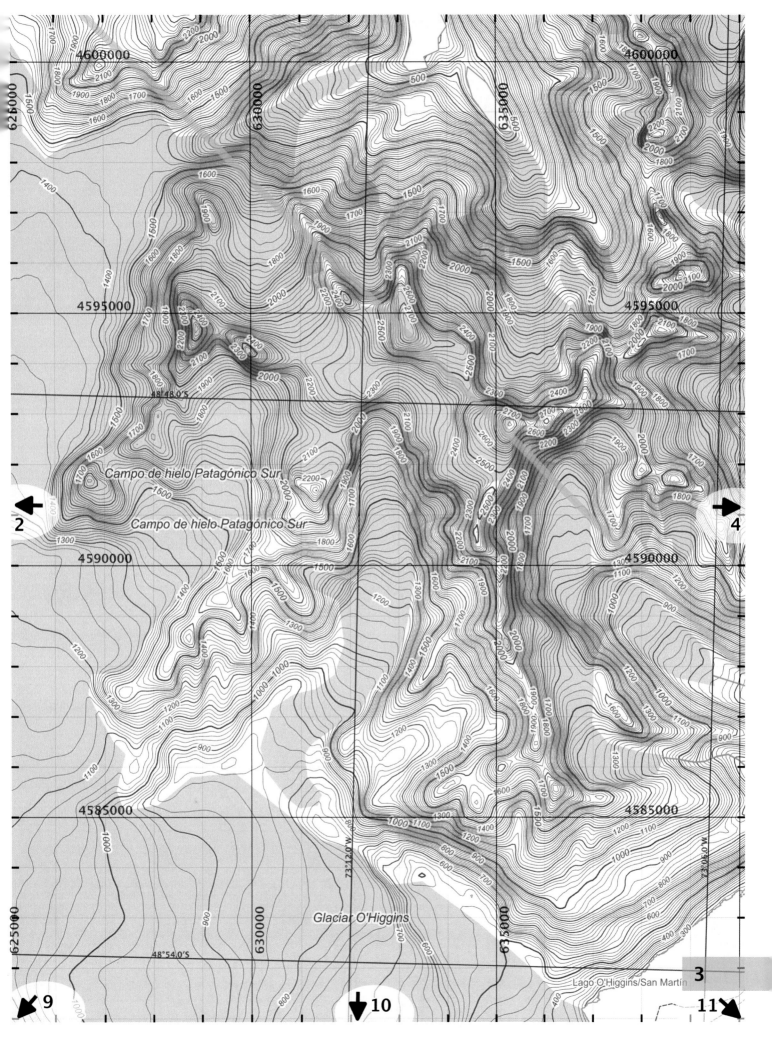

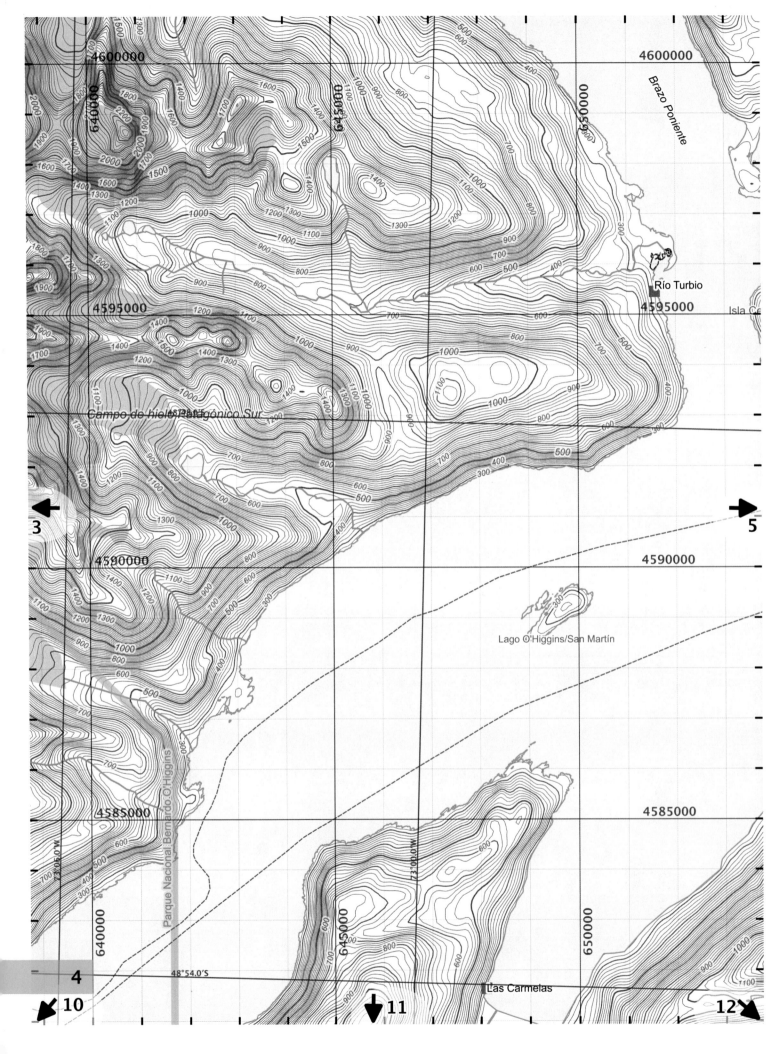

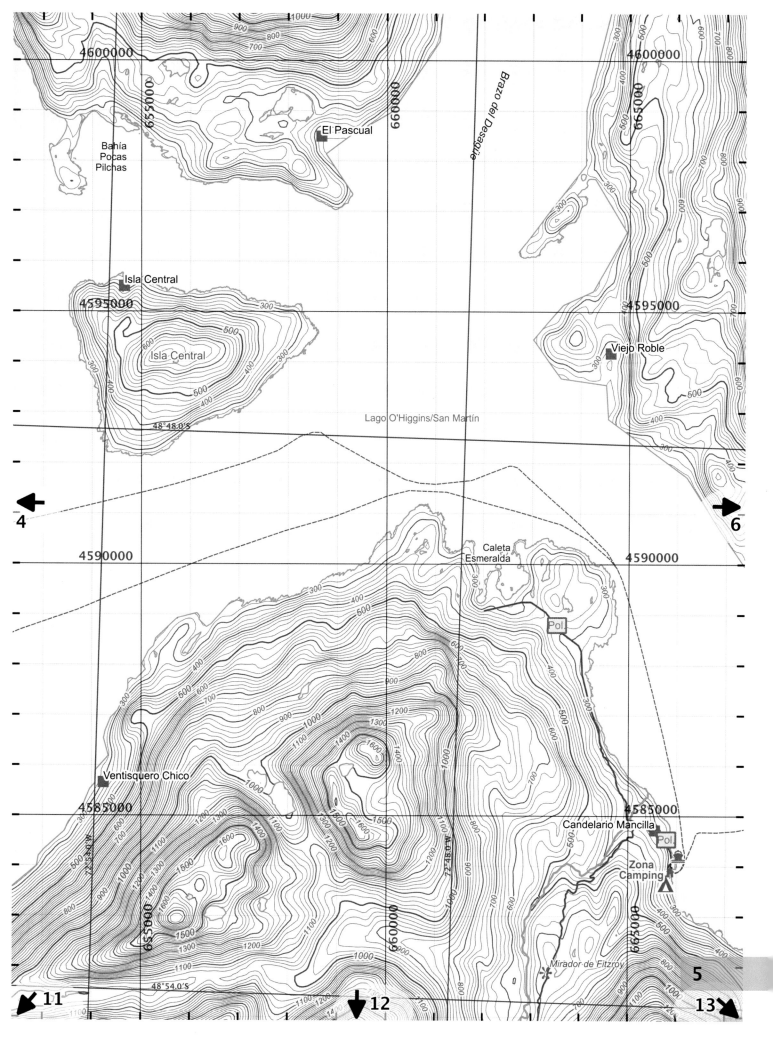

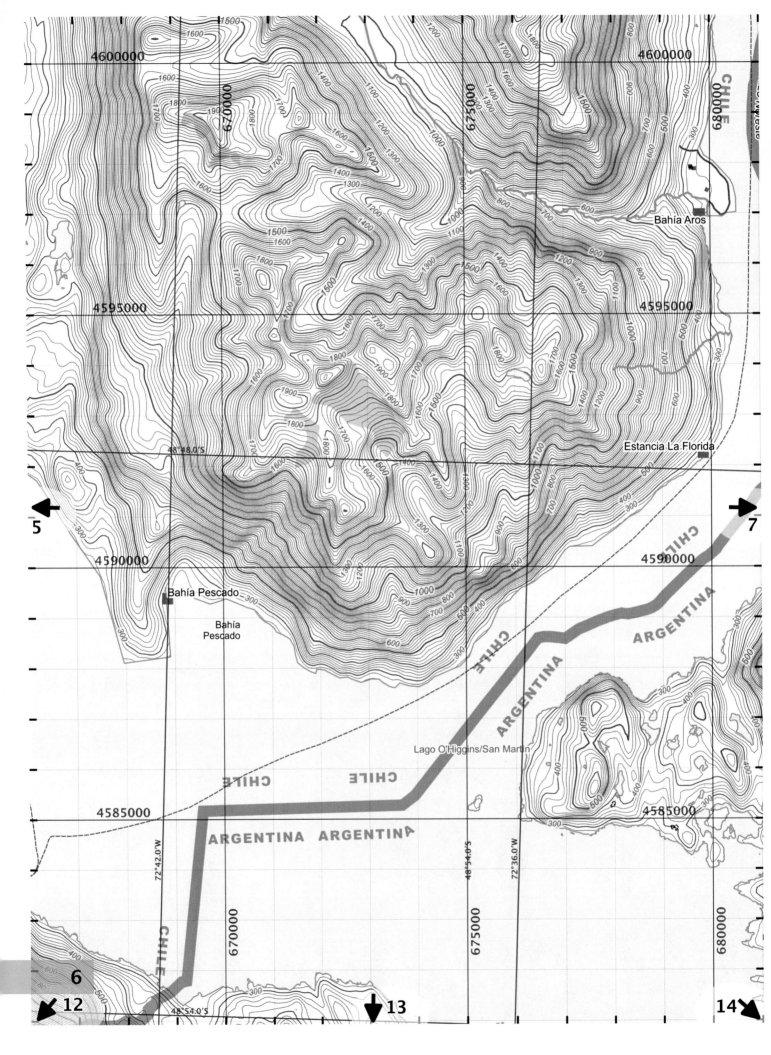

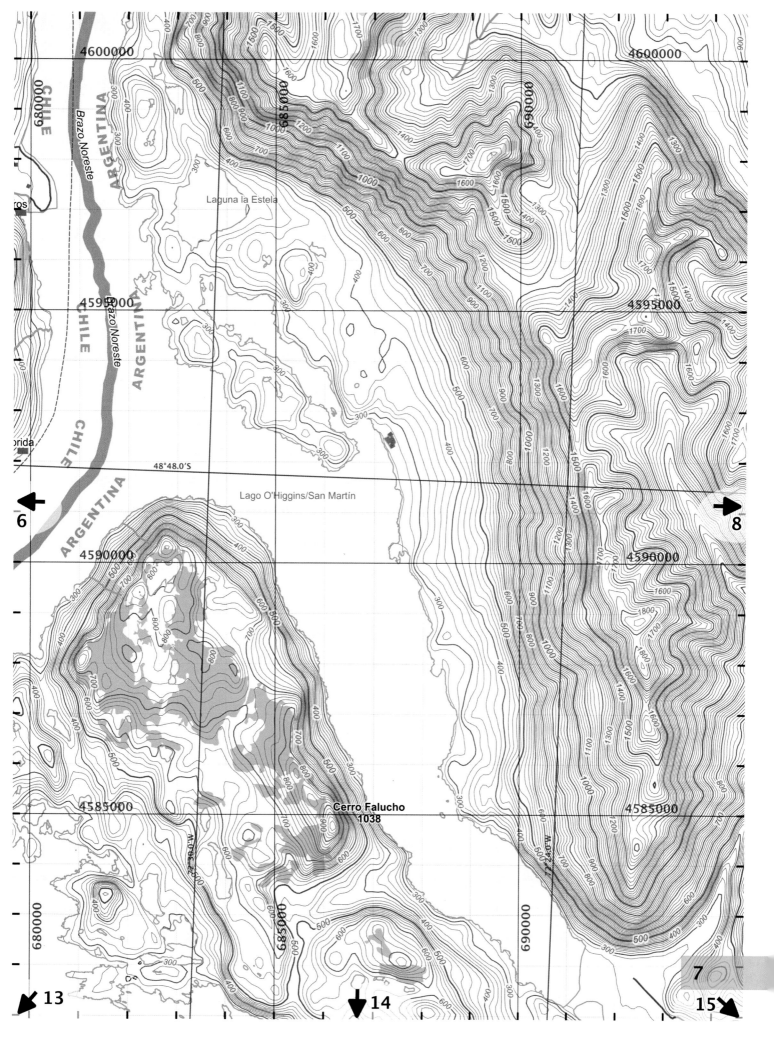

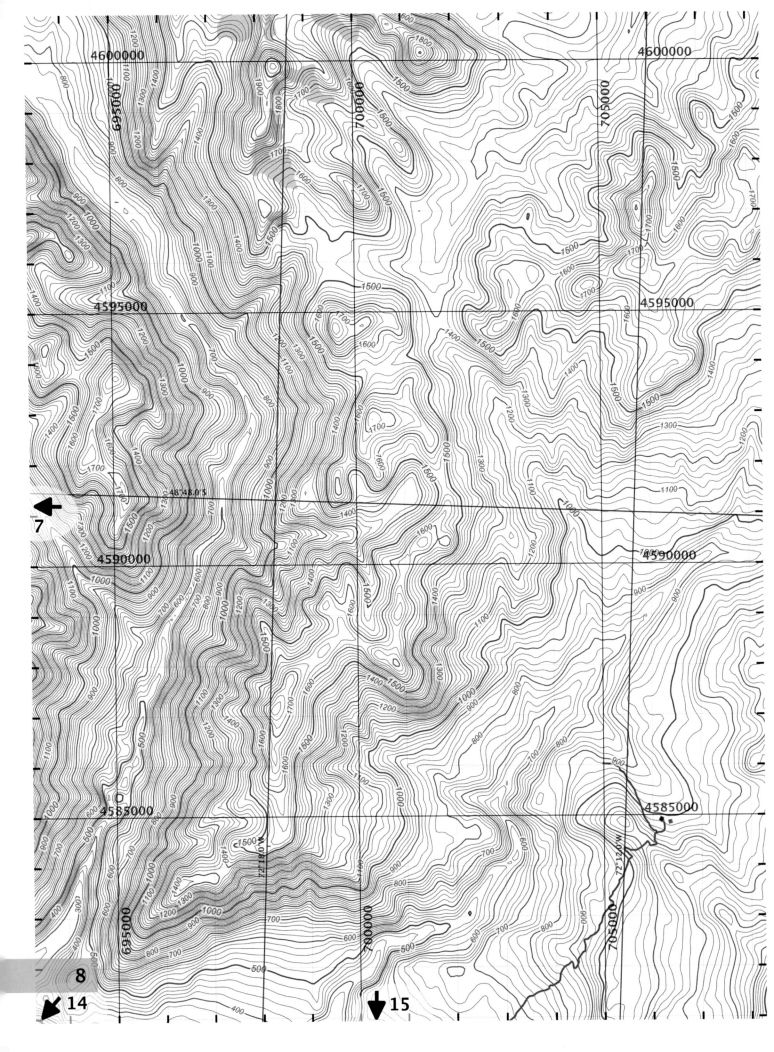

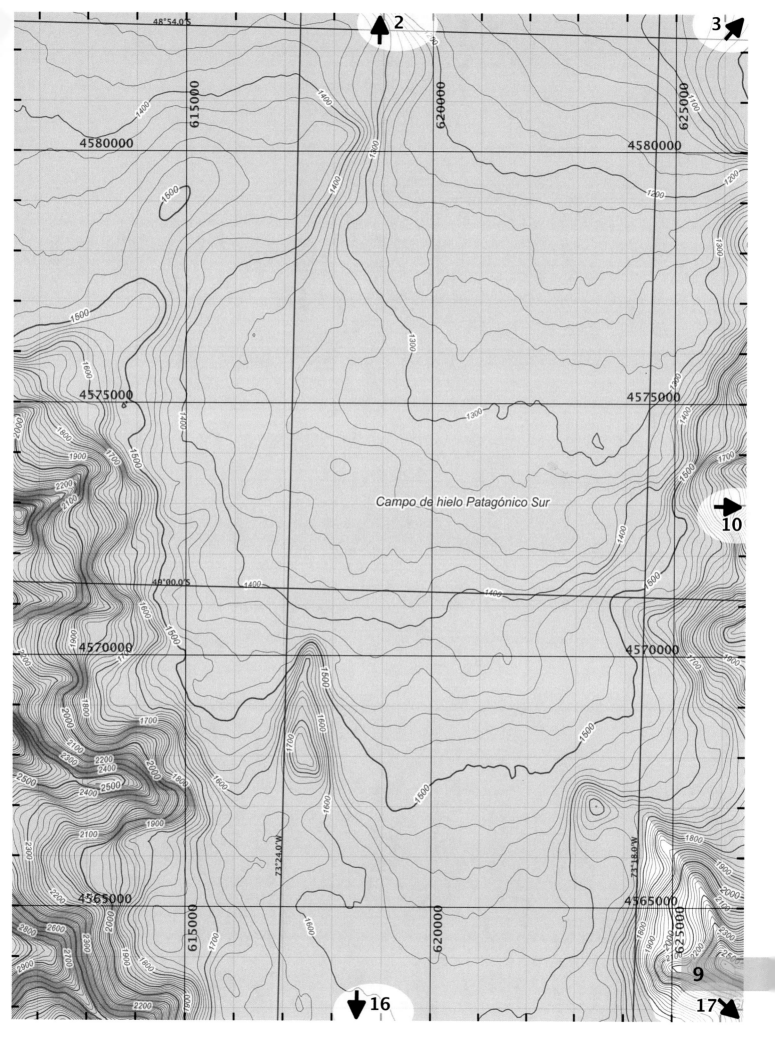

Campo de hielo Patagónico Sur

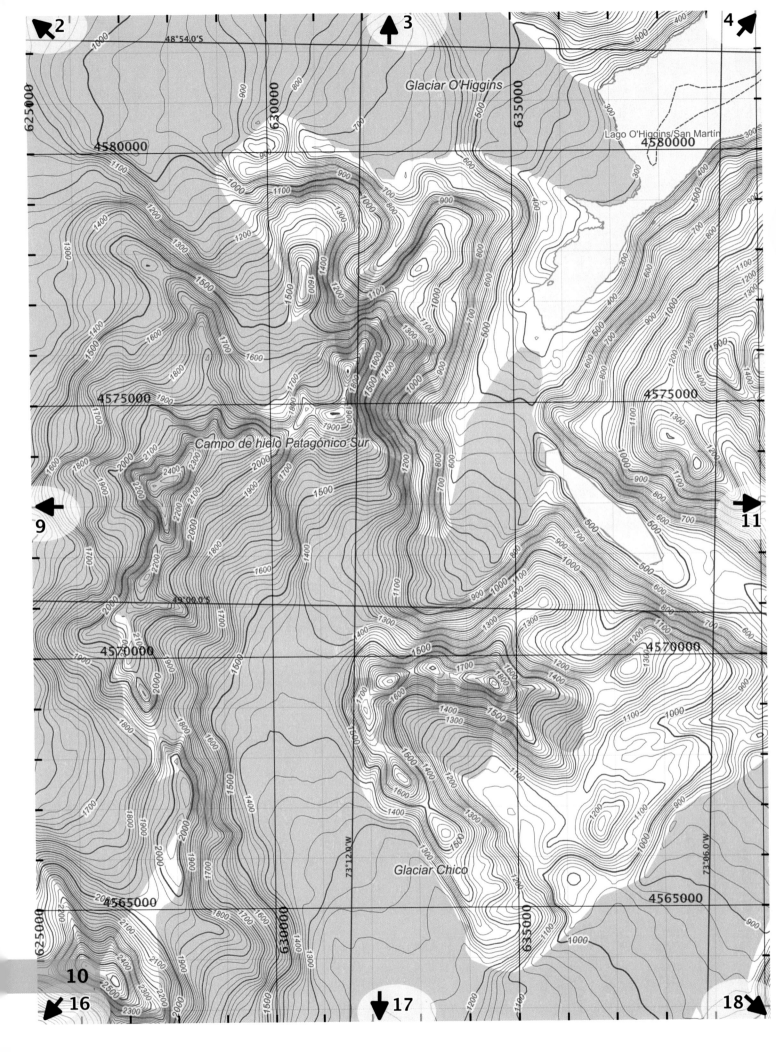

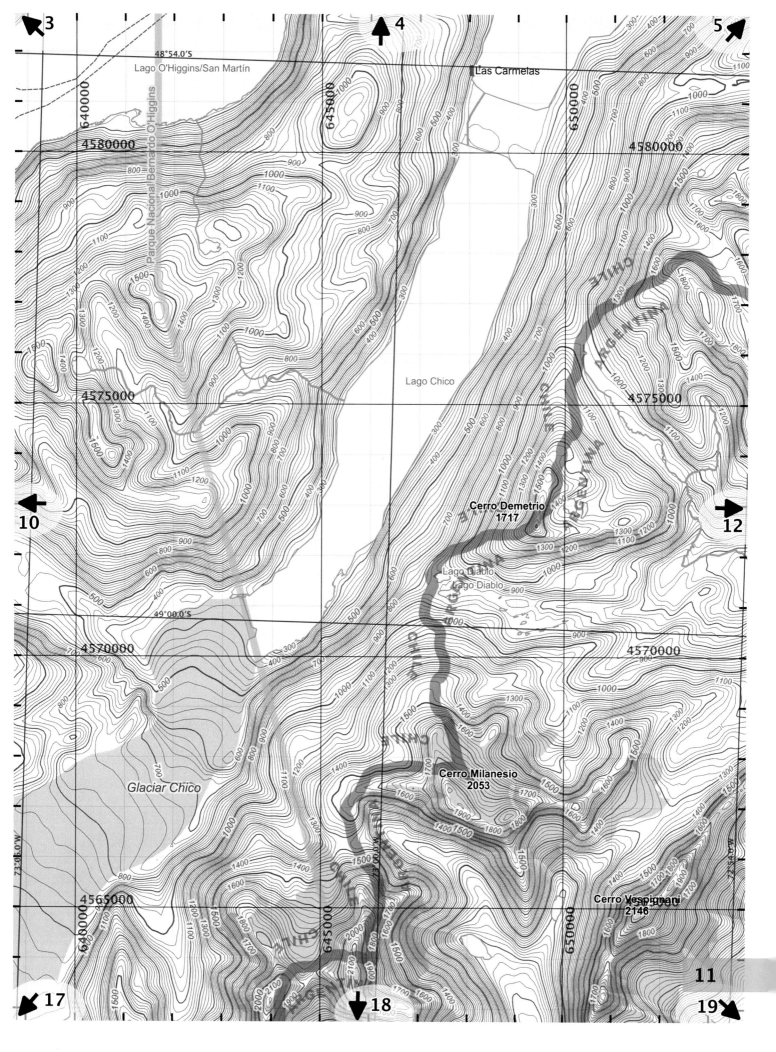

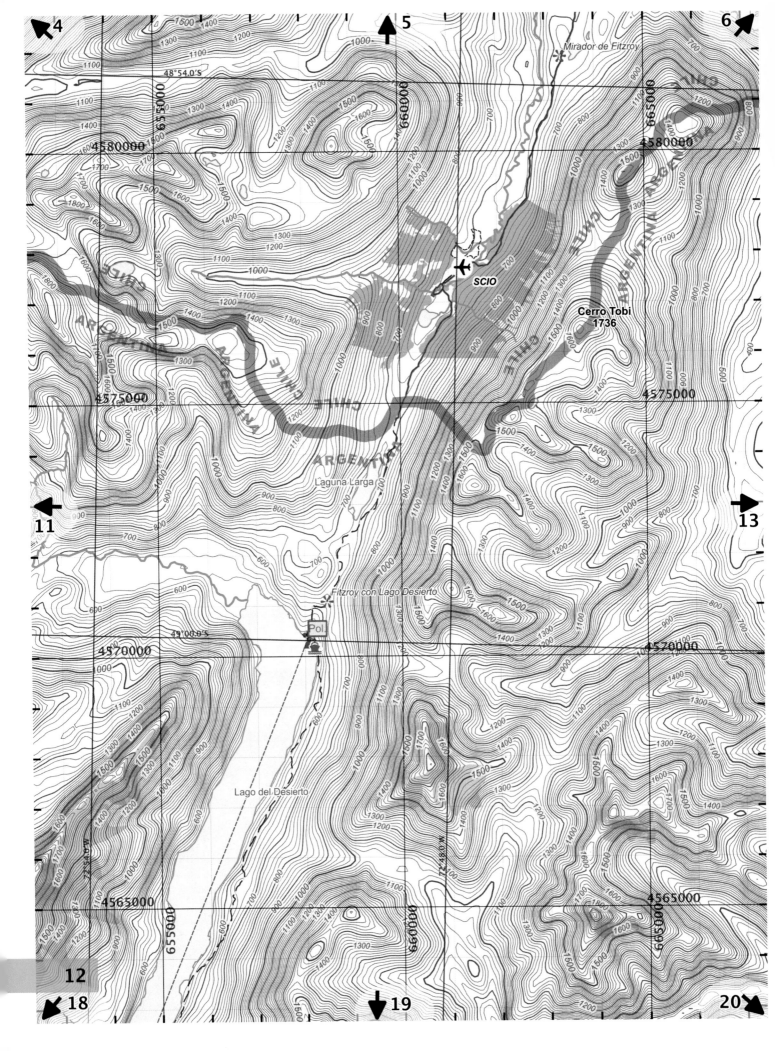

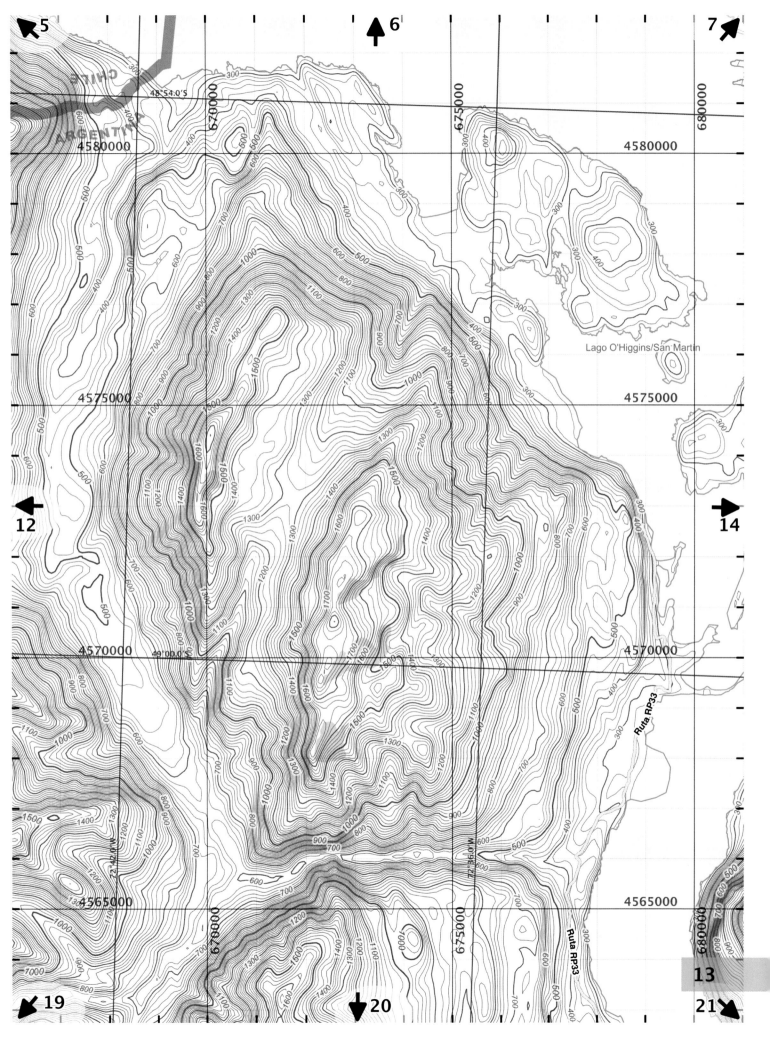

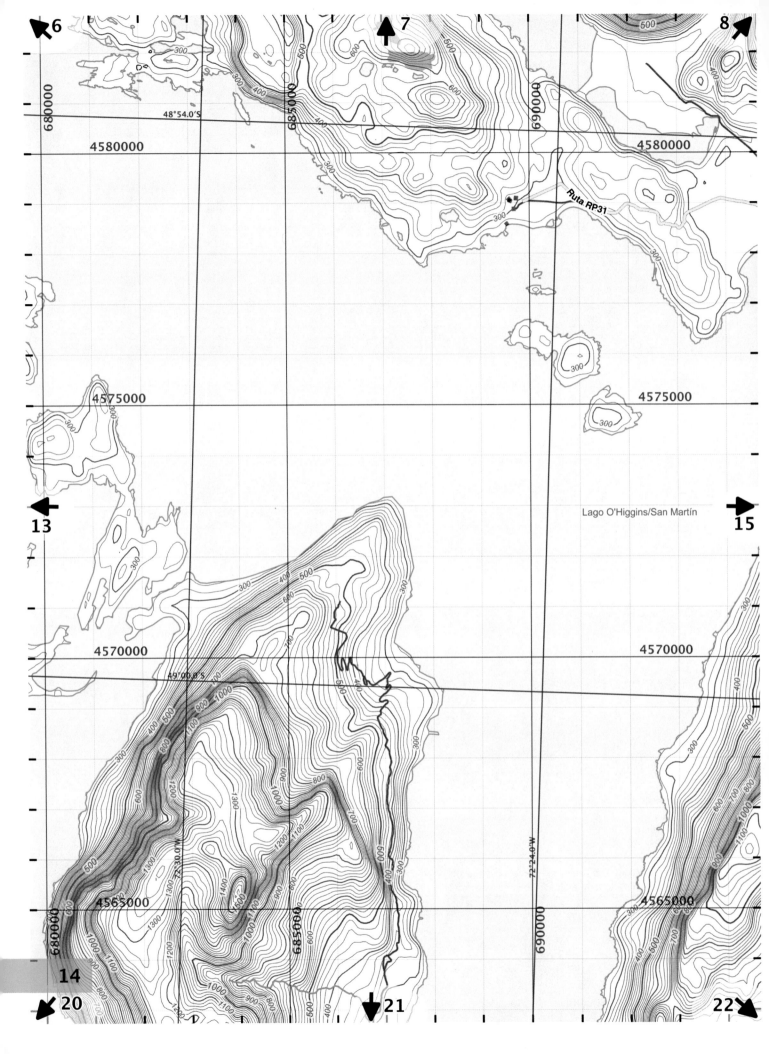

6

7

8

680000

48°54.0'S

4580000

685000

690000

4580000

Ruta RP31

300

300

300

300

4575000

4575000

300

13

Lago O'Higgins/San Martín

15

4570000

49°00.0'S

4570000

72°30.0'W

72°24.0'W

14

4565000

690000

4565000

680000

685000

20

21

22

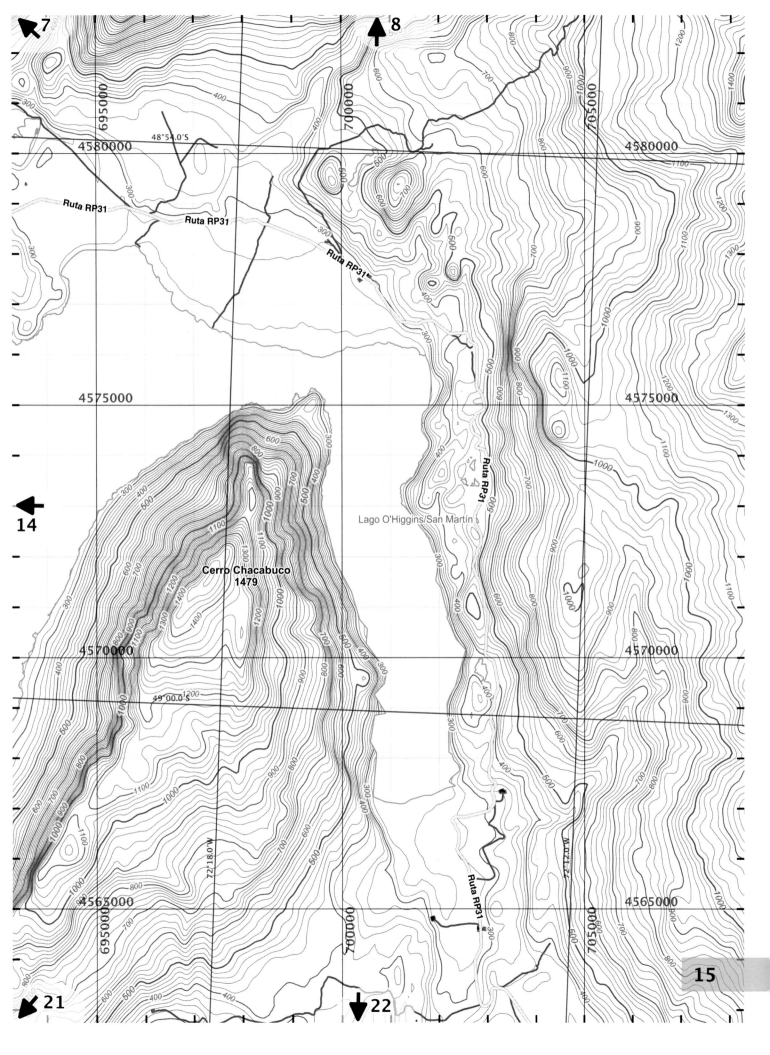

48°54.0'S

695000

4580000

700000

705000

4580000

Ruta RP31

Ruta RP31

Ruta RP31

4575000

4575000

14

Lago O'Higgins/San Martin

Ruta RP31

Cerro Chacabuco
1479

4570000

4570000

49°00.0'S

72°18.0'W

Ruta RP31

72°12.0'W

4565000

4565000

695000

700000

705000

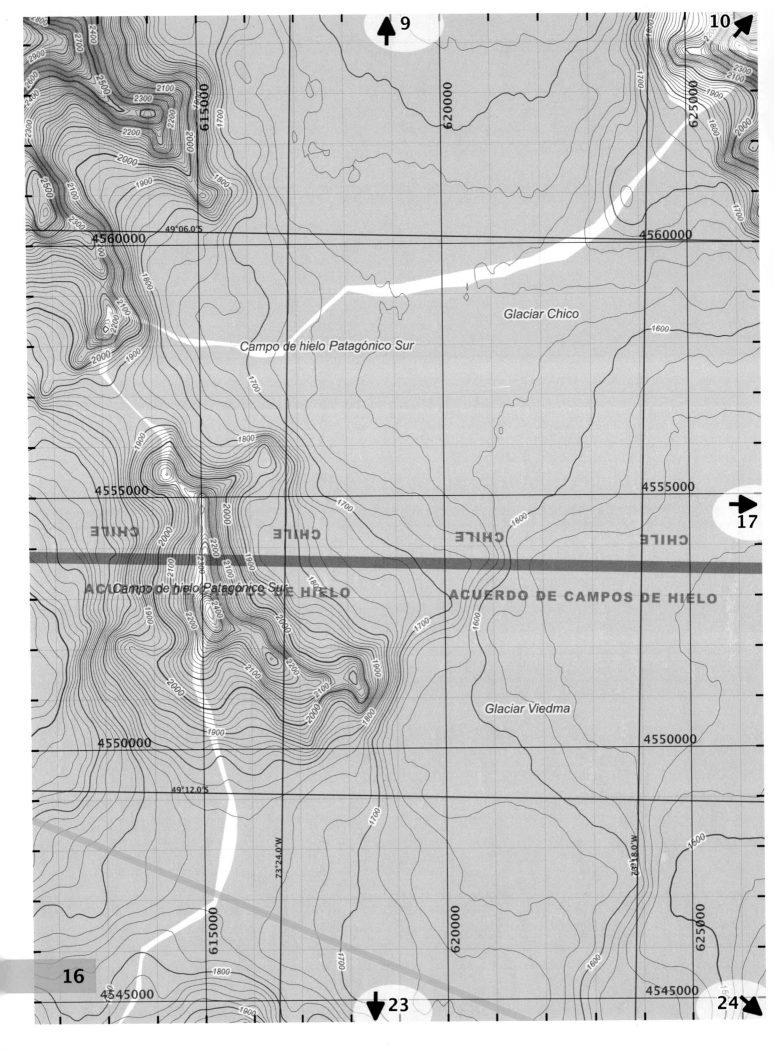

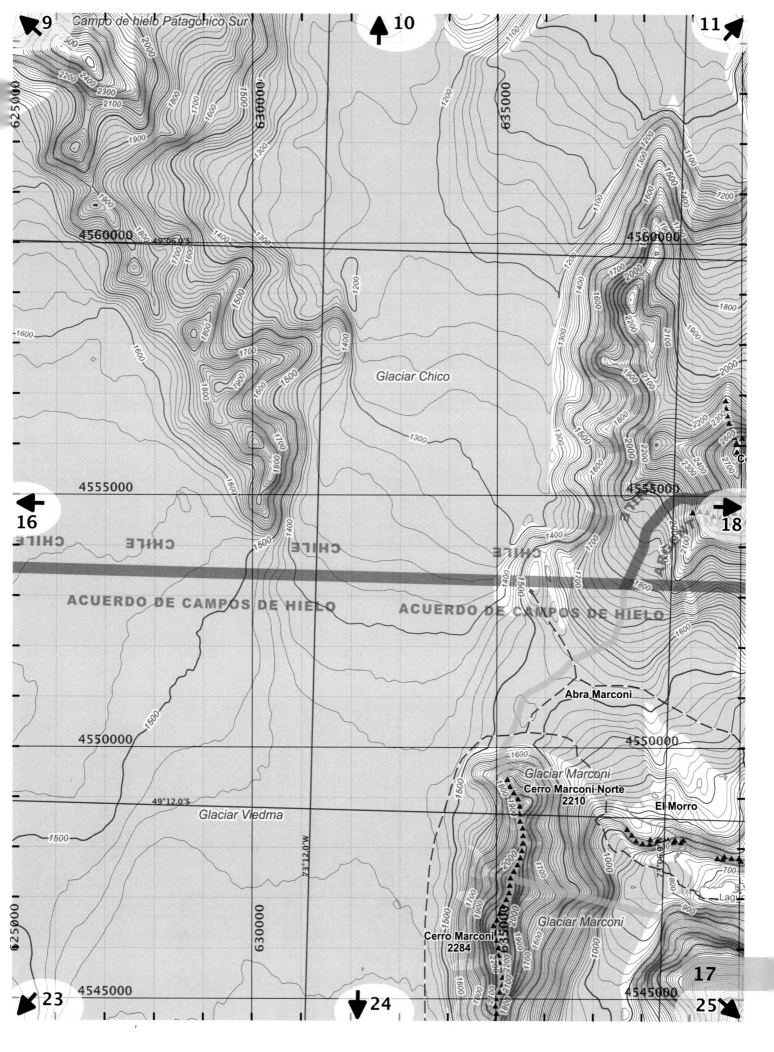

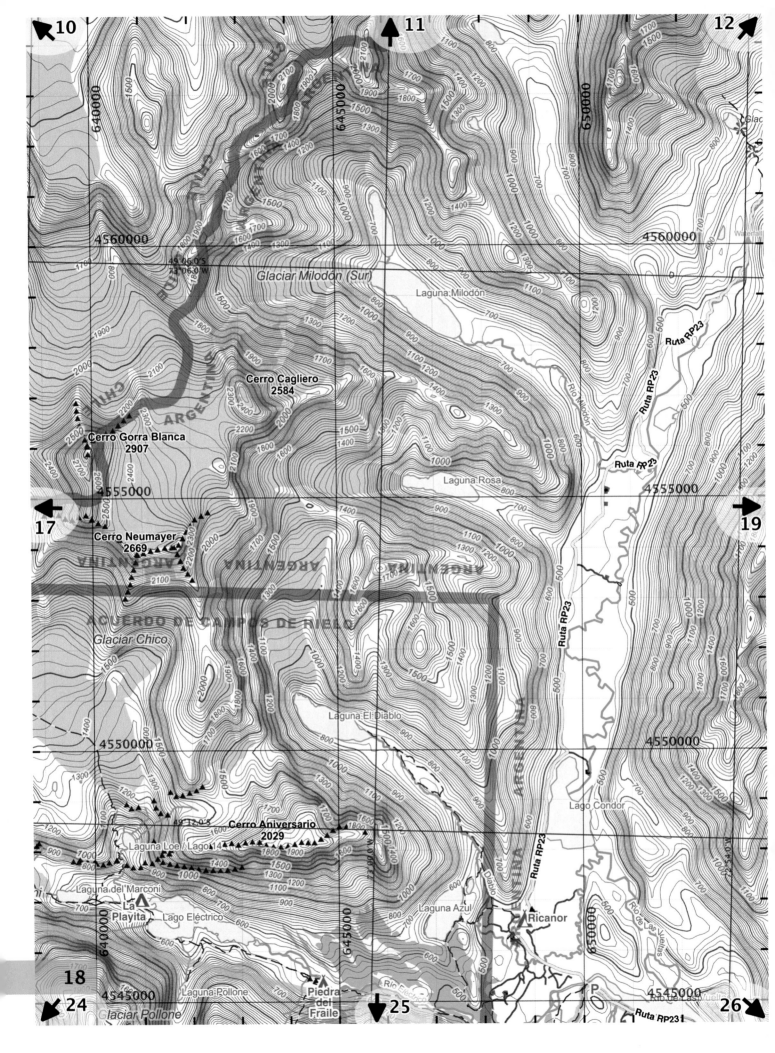

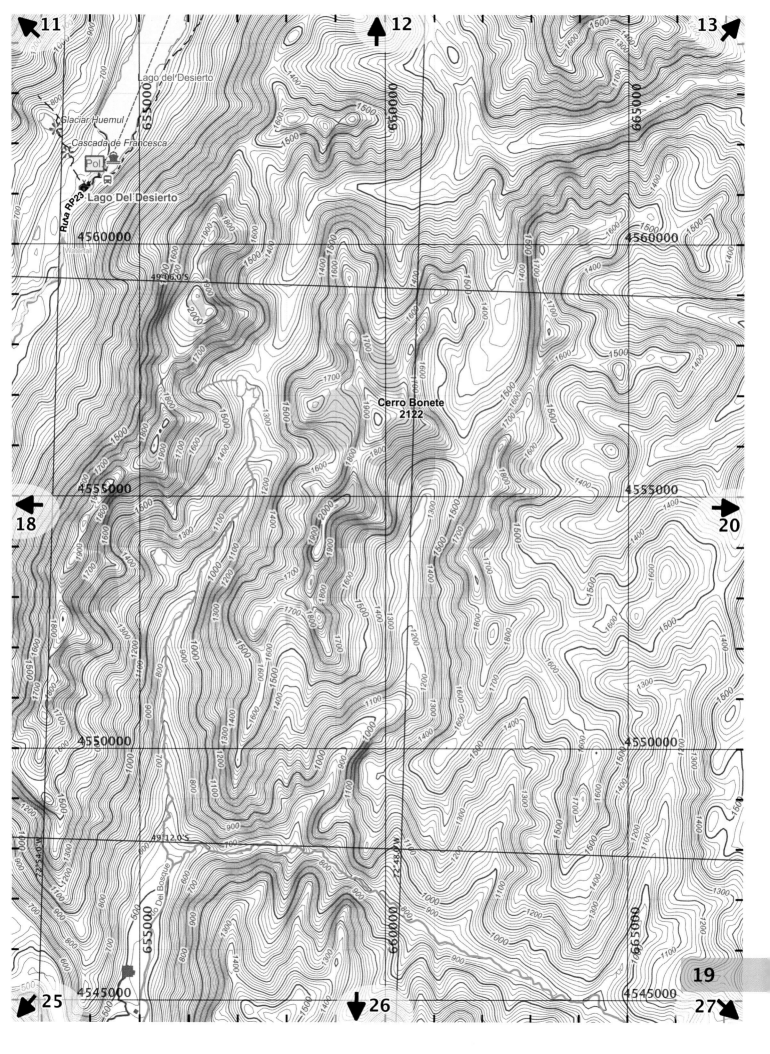

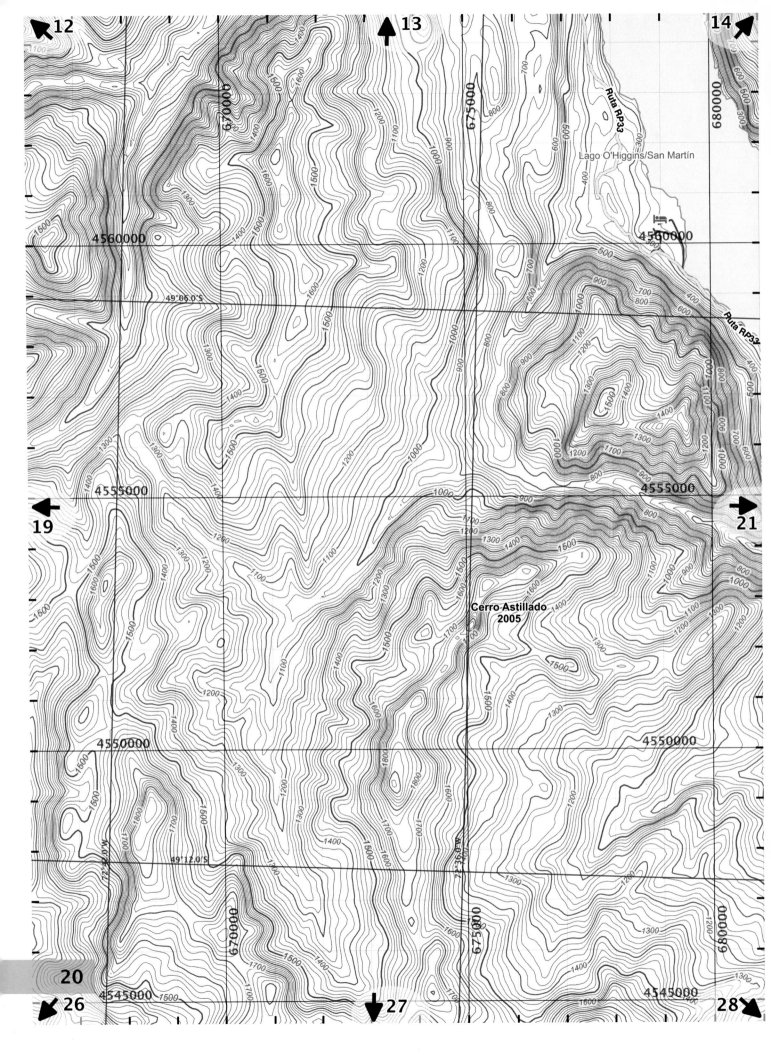

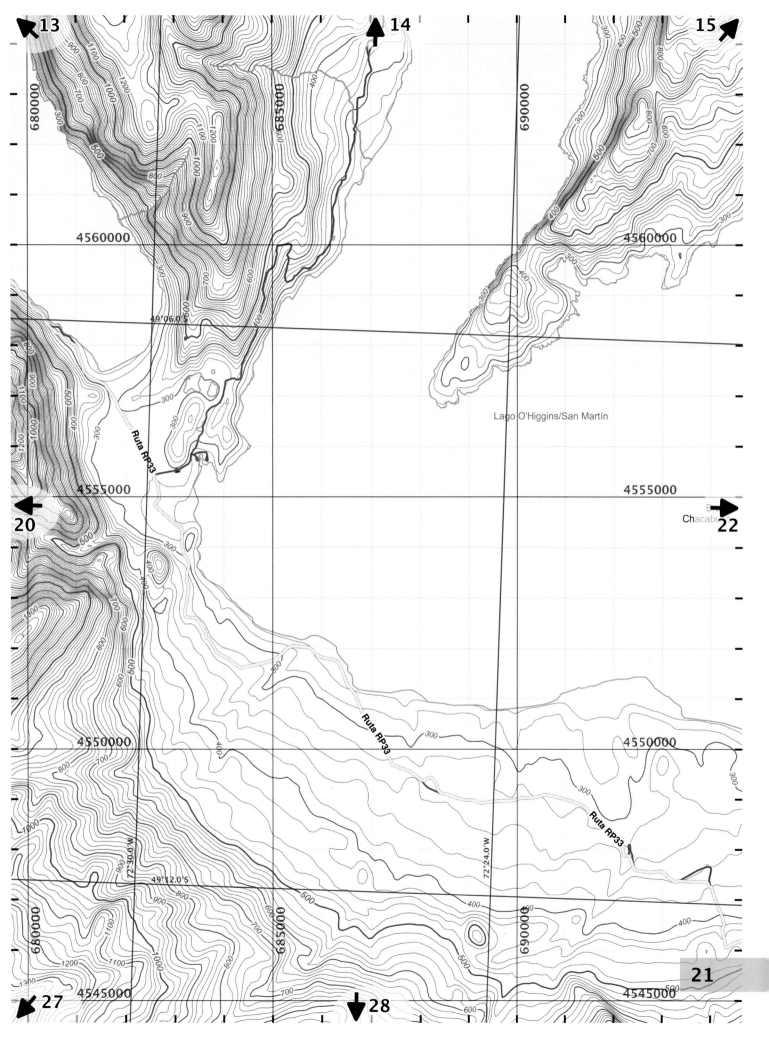

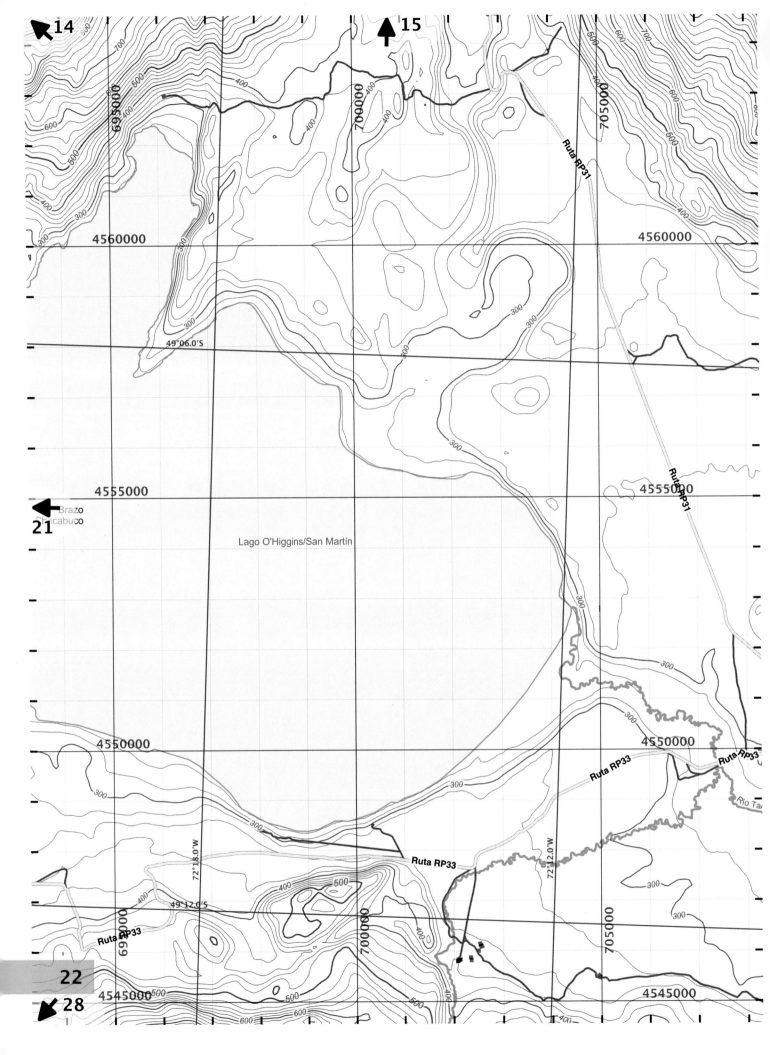

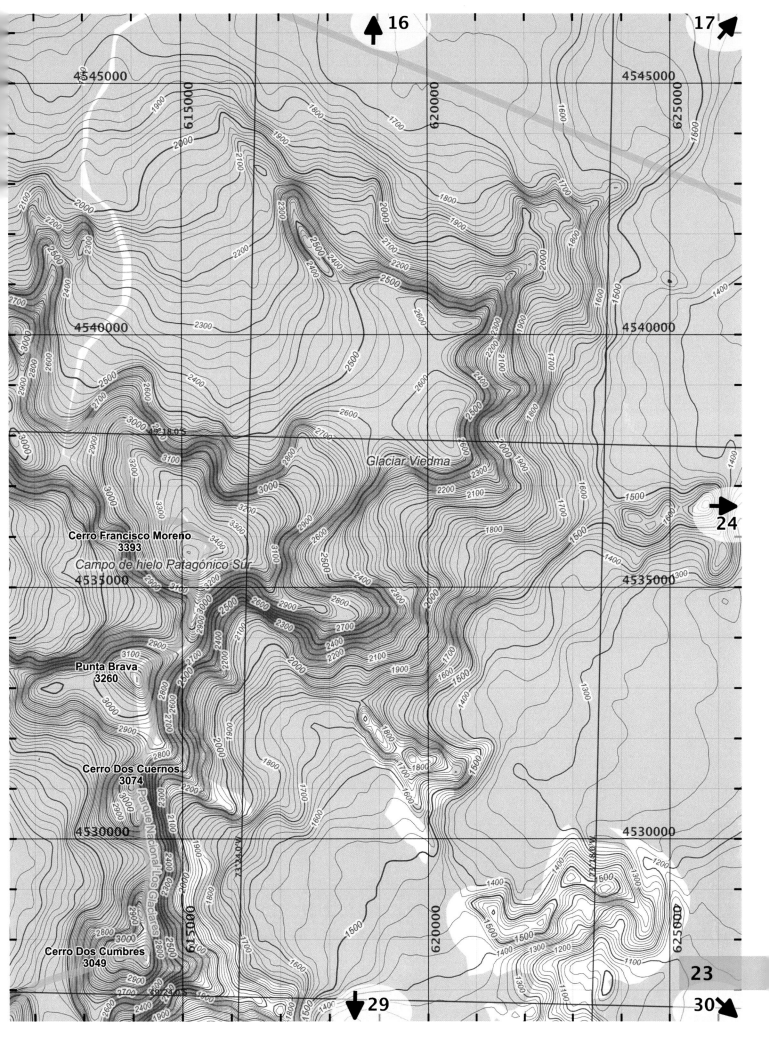

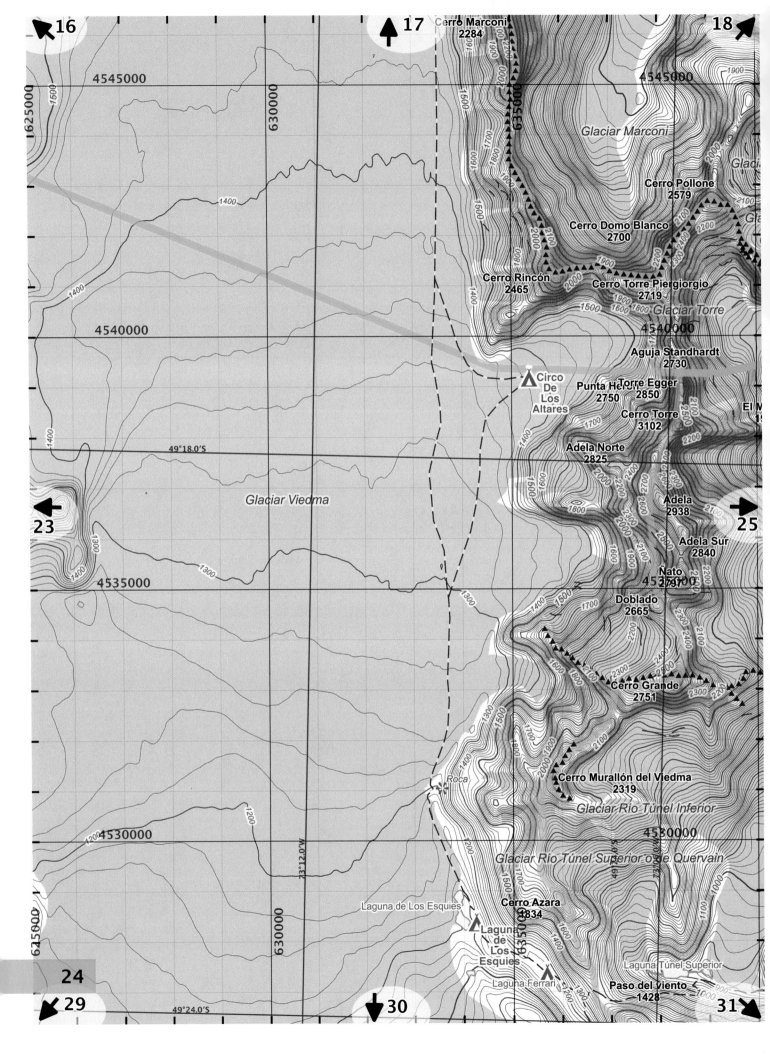

Cerro Marconi
2284

Glaciar Marconi

Cerro Pollone
2579

Cerro Domo Blanco
2700

Cerro Rincón
2465

Cerro Torre Piergiorgio
2719

Glaciar Torre

4545000

4540000

1625000

630000

1400

1400

1500

1400

1400

Aguja Standhardt
2730

△ Circo
De
Los
Altares

Punta H
2750

Torre Egger
2850

El M

Cerro Torre
3102

Adela Norte
2825

49°18.0'S

Glaciar Viedma

Adela
2938

Adela Sur
2840

Ñato
2797

4535000

Doblado
2665

Cerro Grande
2751

Roca

Cerro Murallón del Viedma
2319

Glaciar Río Túnel Inferior

4530000

1200 4530000

Glaciar Río Túnel Superior o de Quervain

49°24.0'S

Laguna de Los Esquies

Cerro Azara
1834

Laguna
de
Los
Esquies

Laguna Túnel Superior

Laguna Ferrari

Paso del Viento
1428

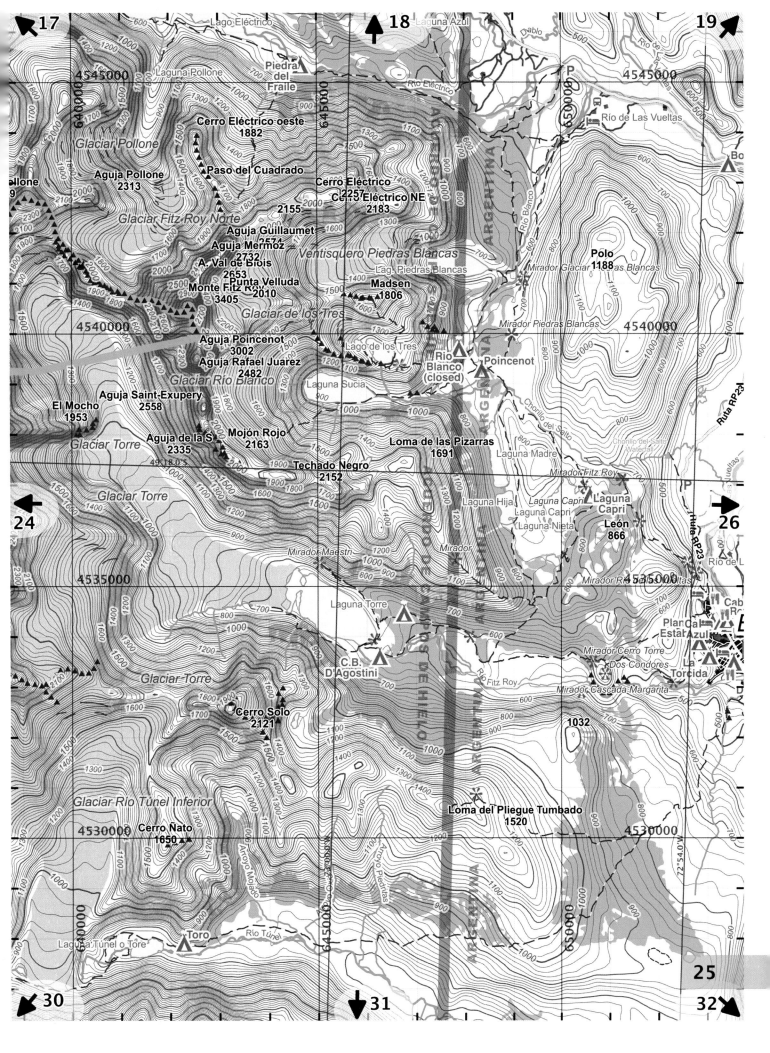

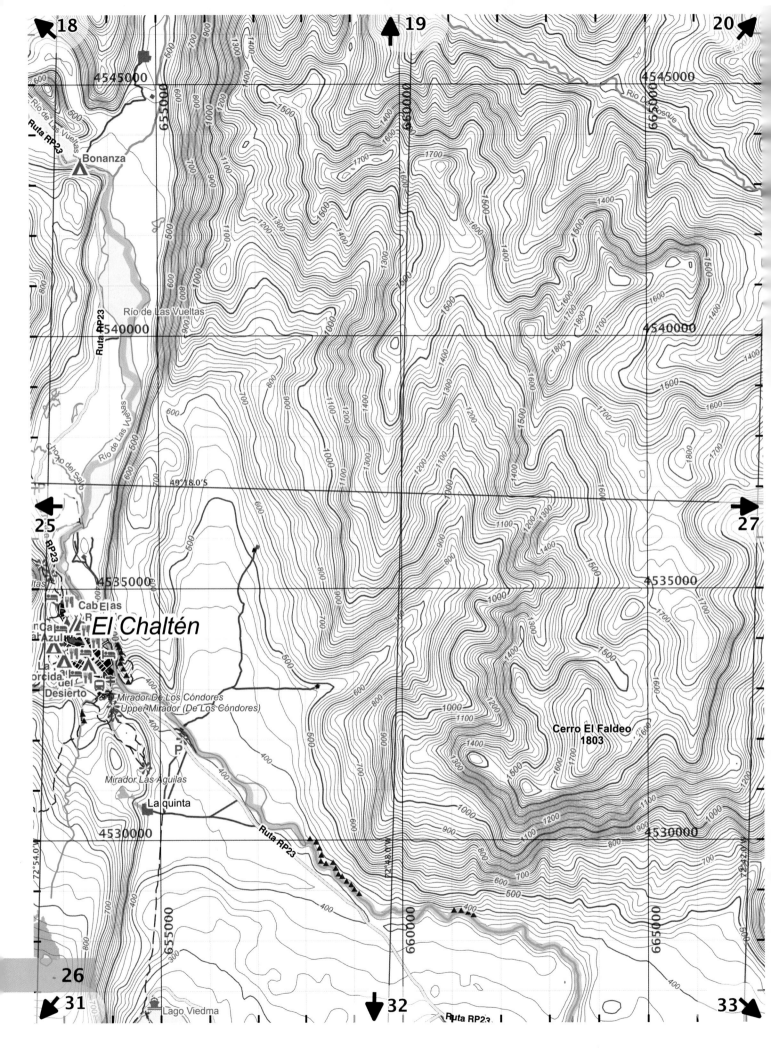

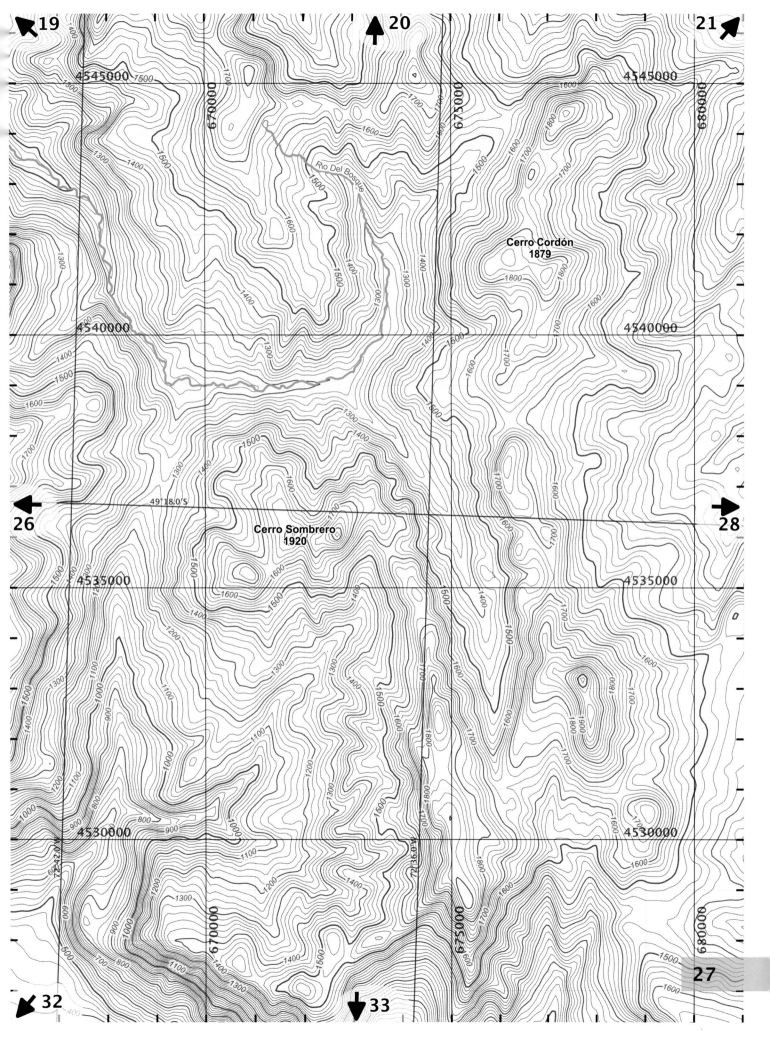

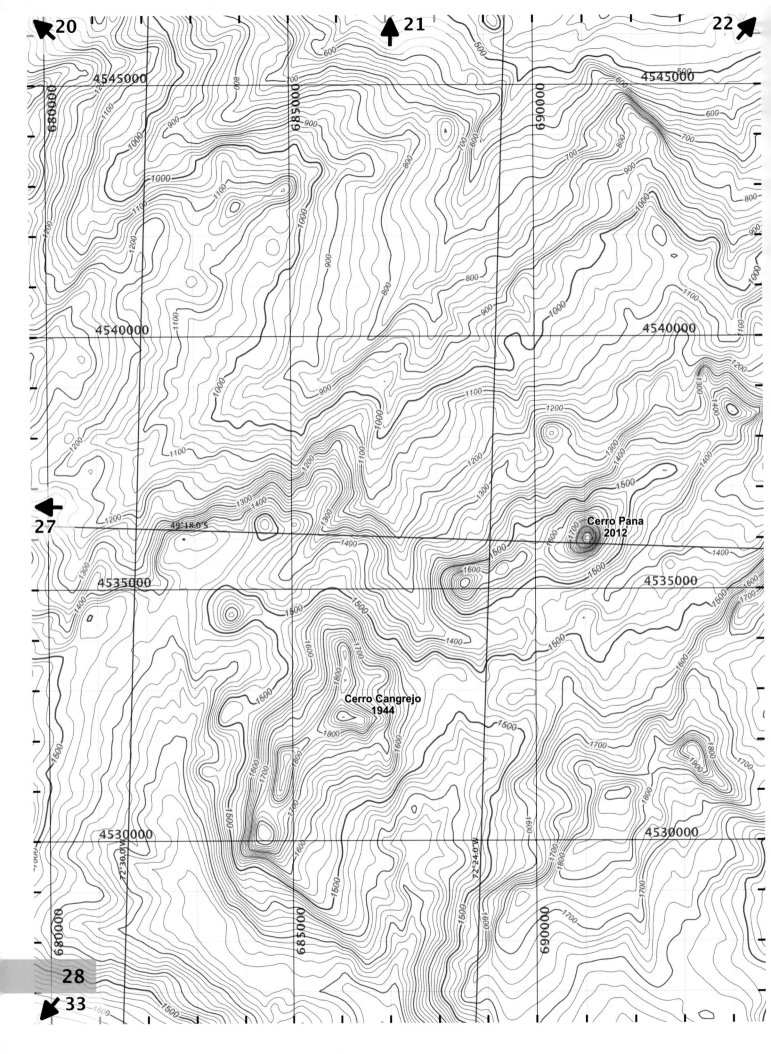

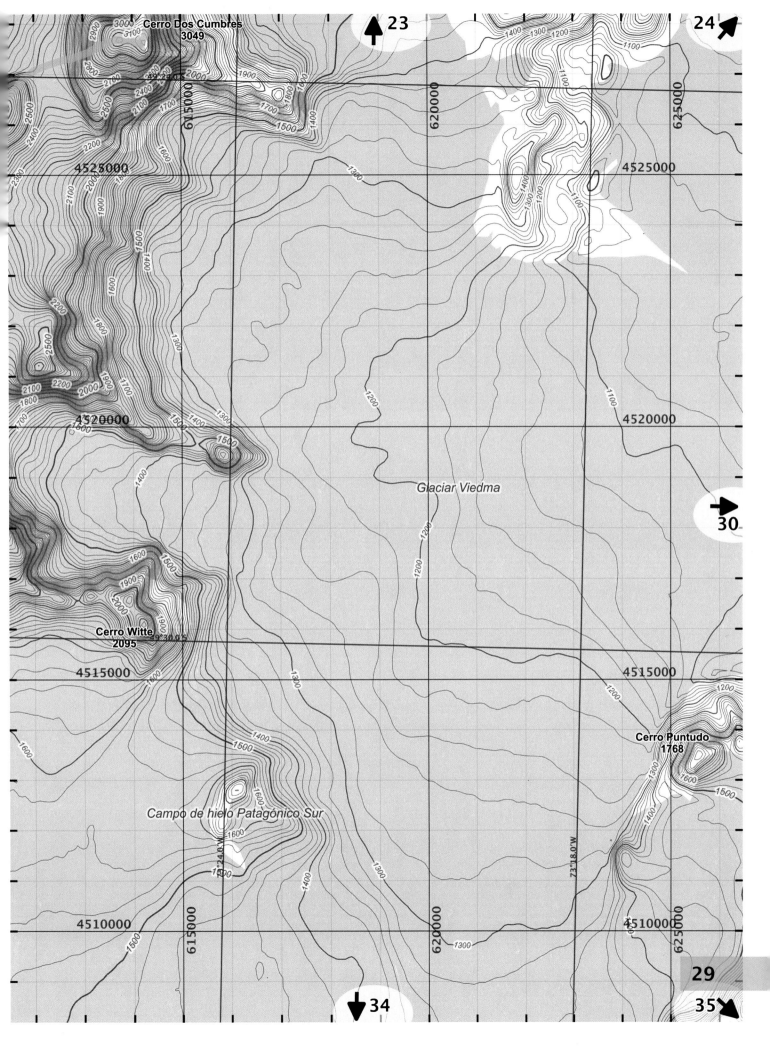

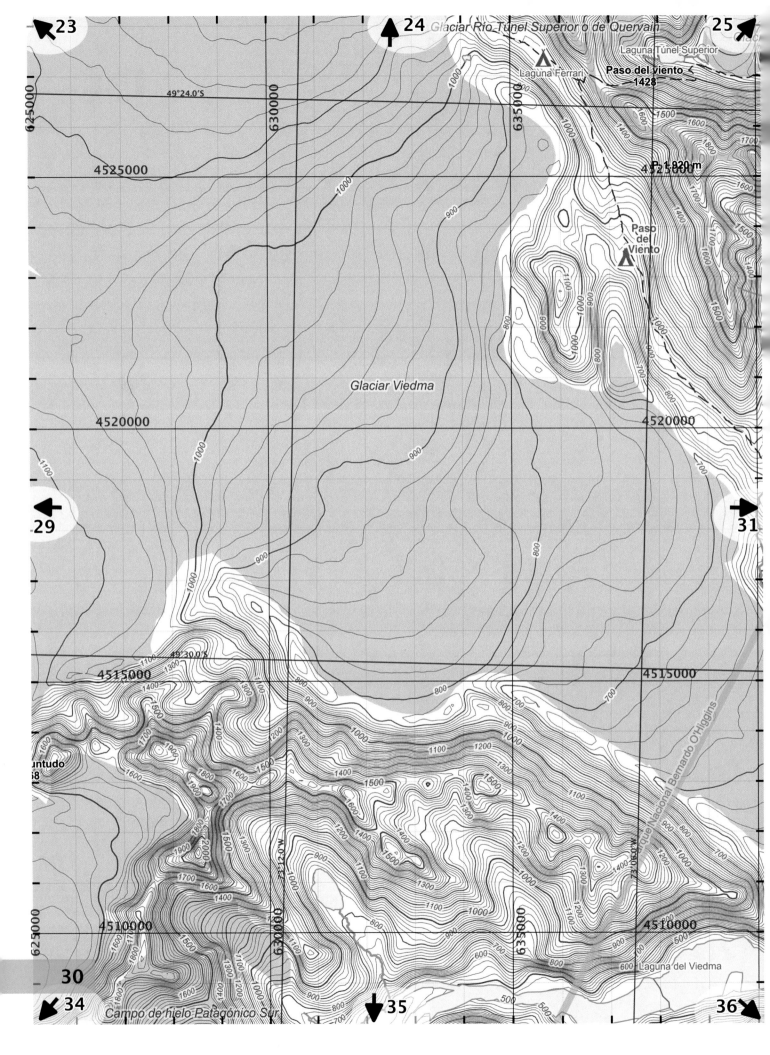

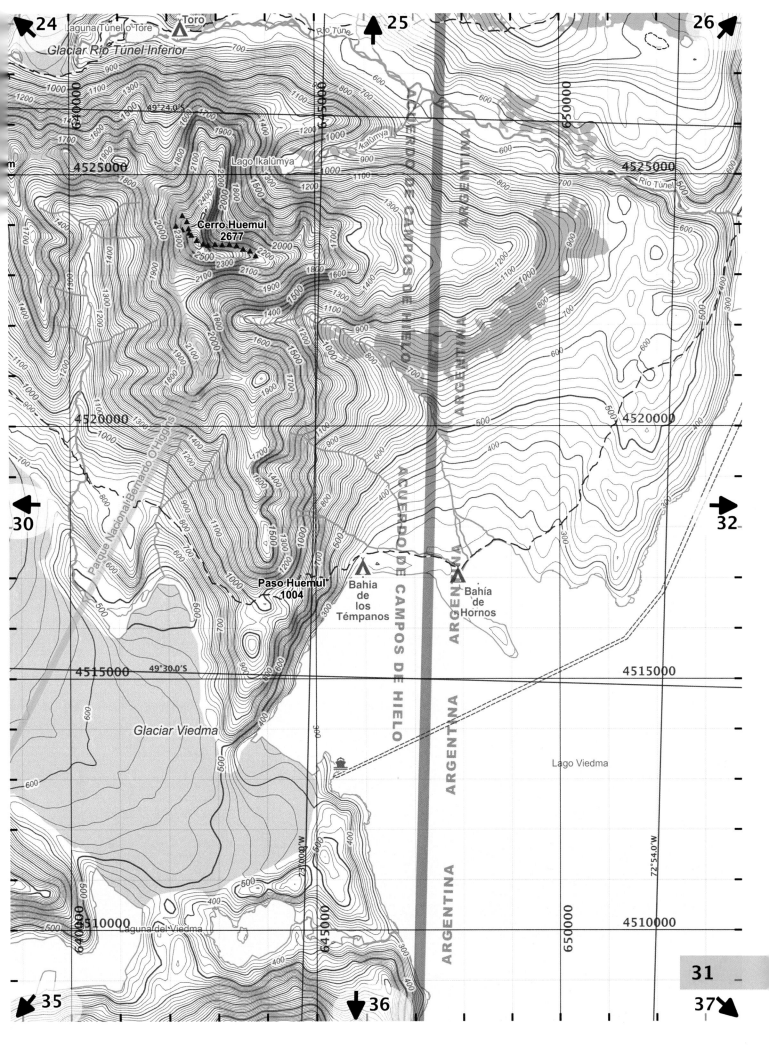

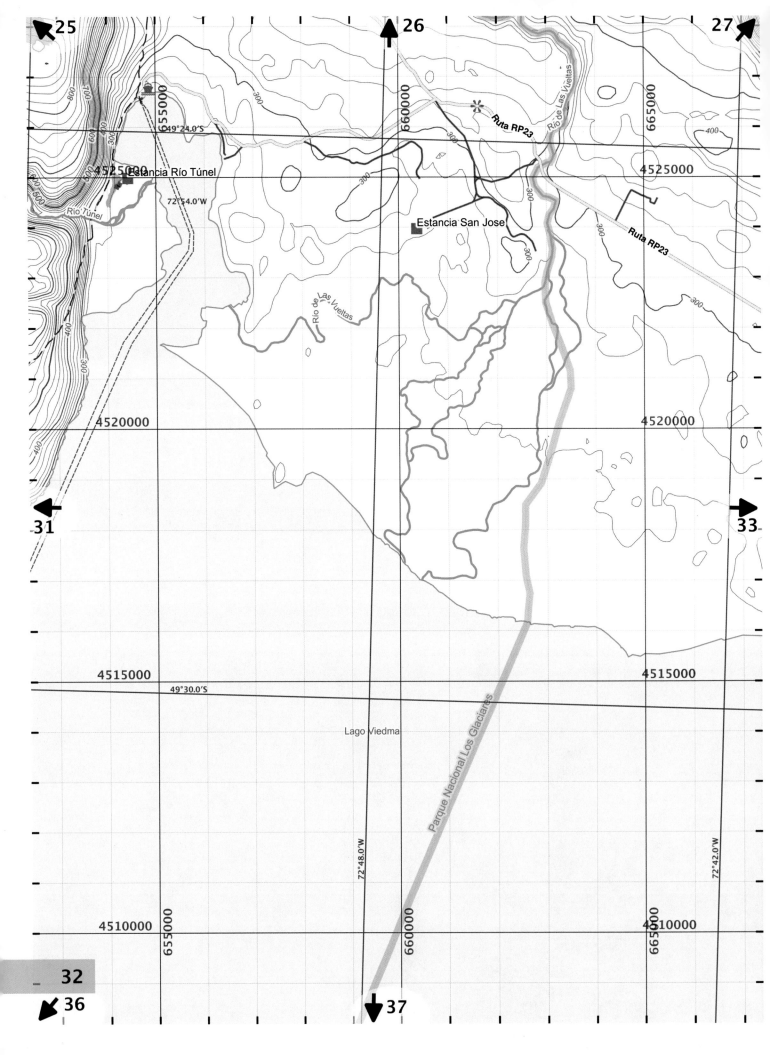

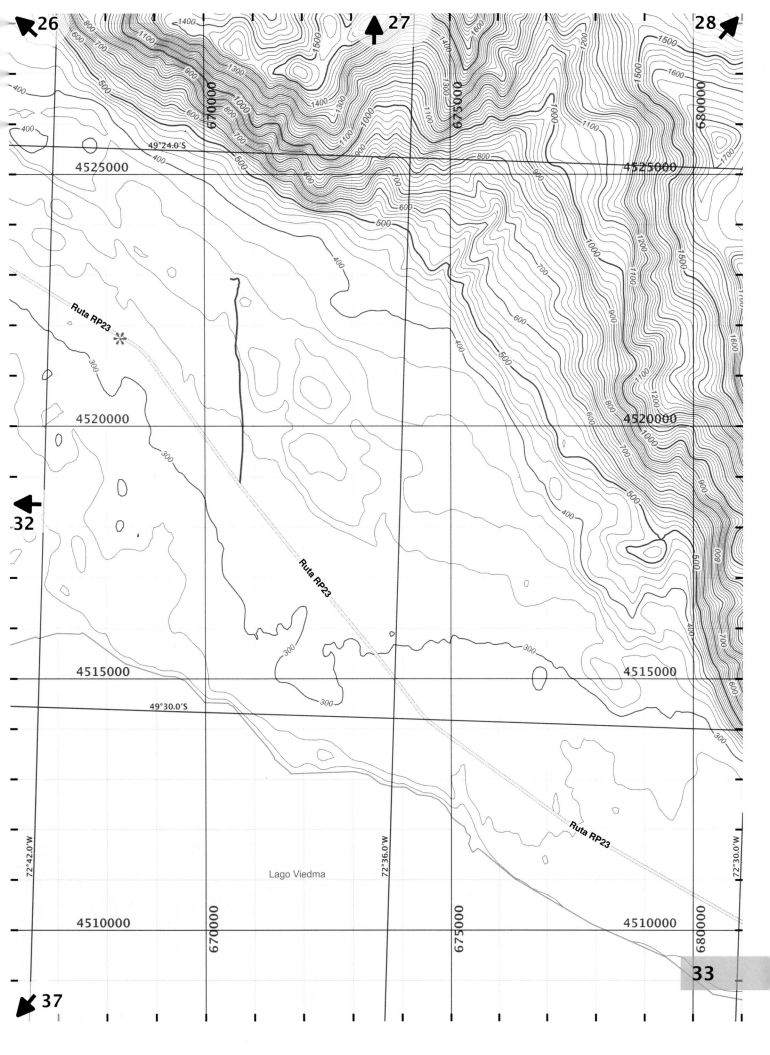

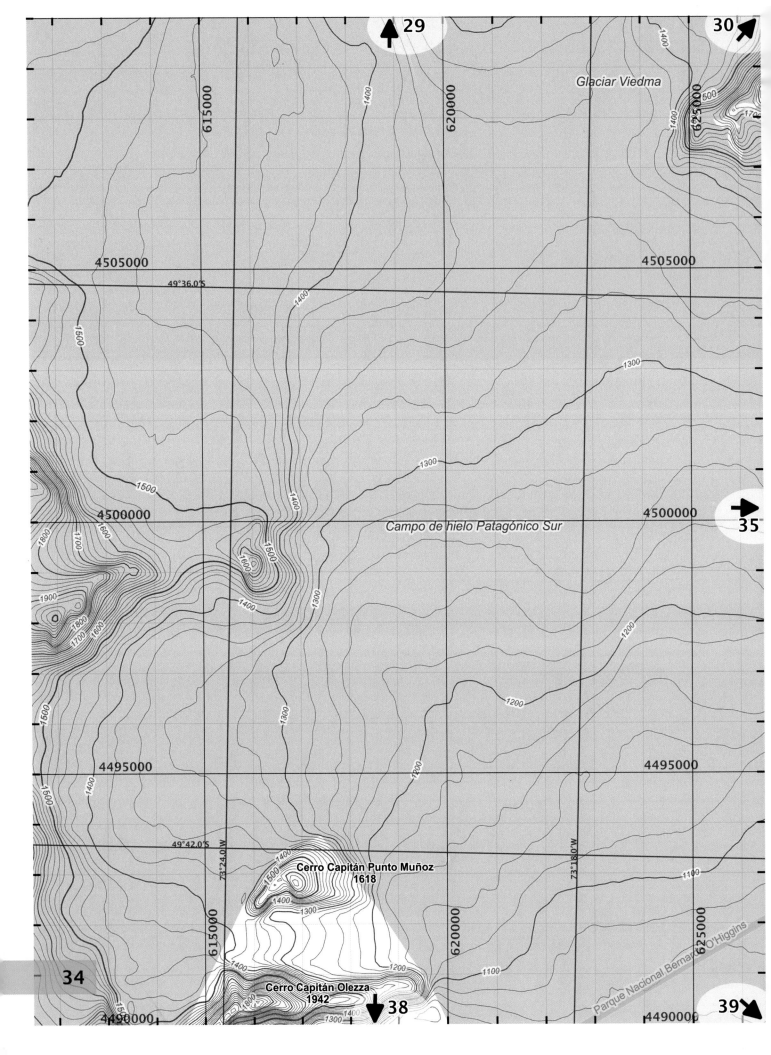

Glaciar Viedma

615000

620000

625000

4505000

4505000

49°36.0'S

1400

1500

1300

4500000

4500000

Campo de hielo Patagónico Sur

1500

1600

1800

1700

1900

1800

1700

1600

1500

1200

1200

4495000

4495000

1200

49°42.0'S

73°24.0'W

615000

73°18.0'W

620000

625000

1100

Cerro Capitán Punto Muñoz
1618

1400

1500

1400

1300

1100

1200

1400

1200

Parque Nacional Bernardo O'Higgins

Cerro Capitán Olezza
1942

1500

1800

1300

1400

4490000

1300

4490000

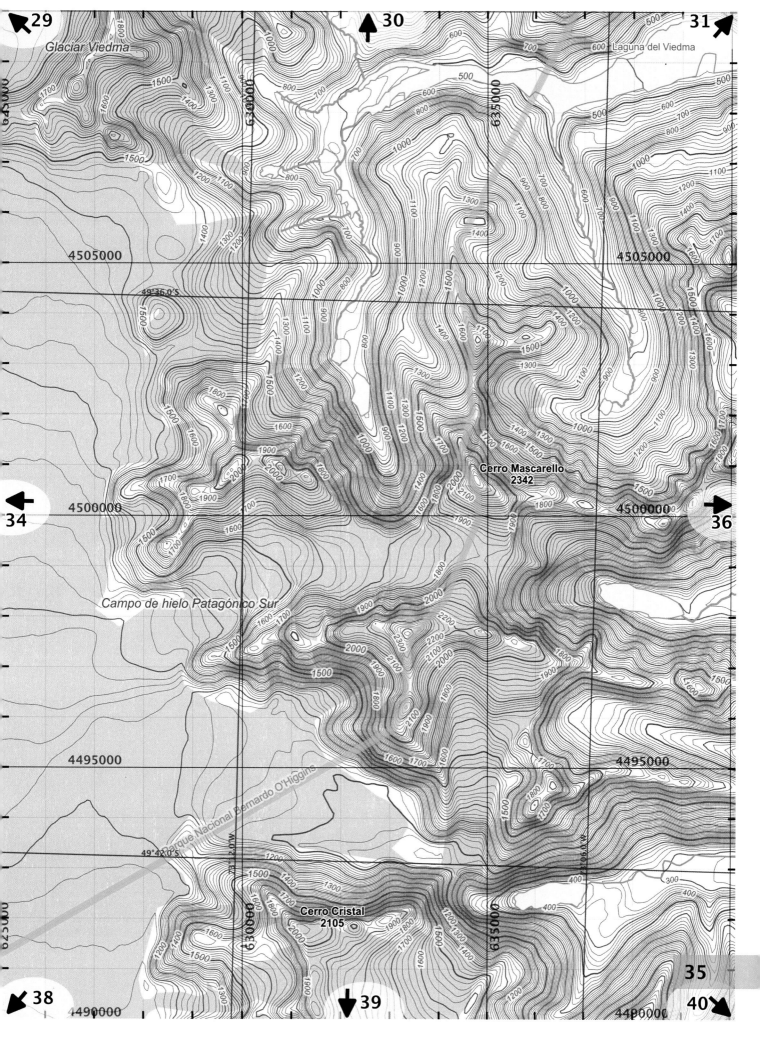

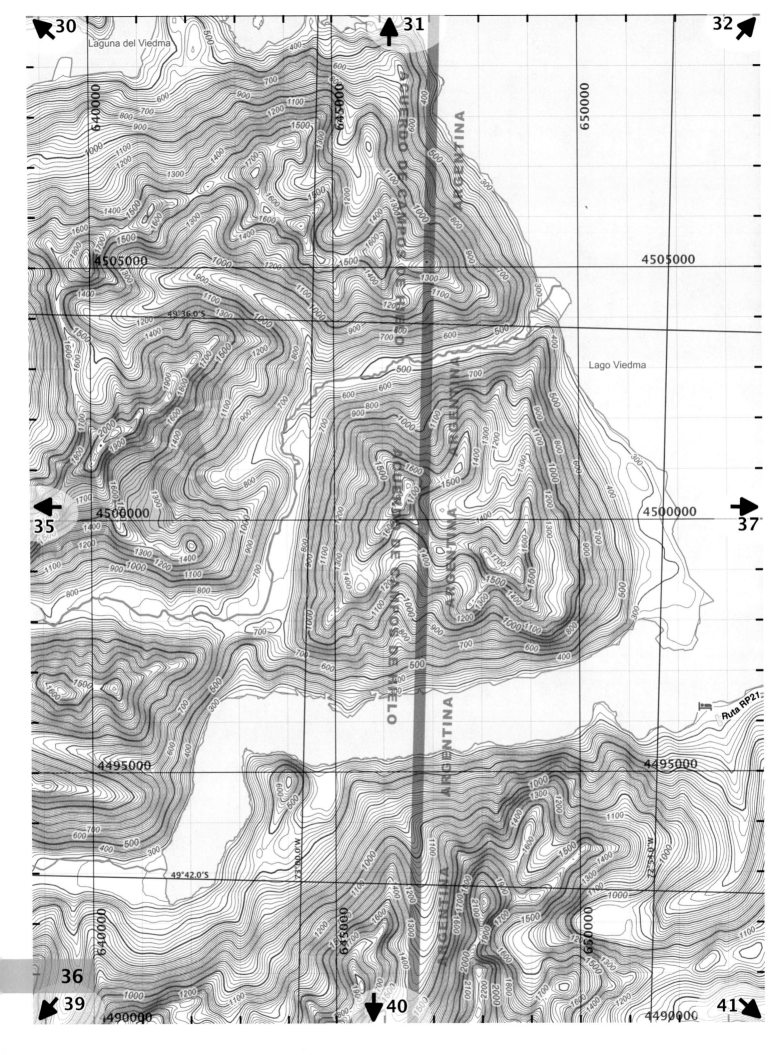

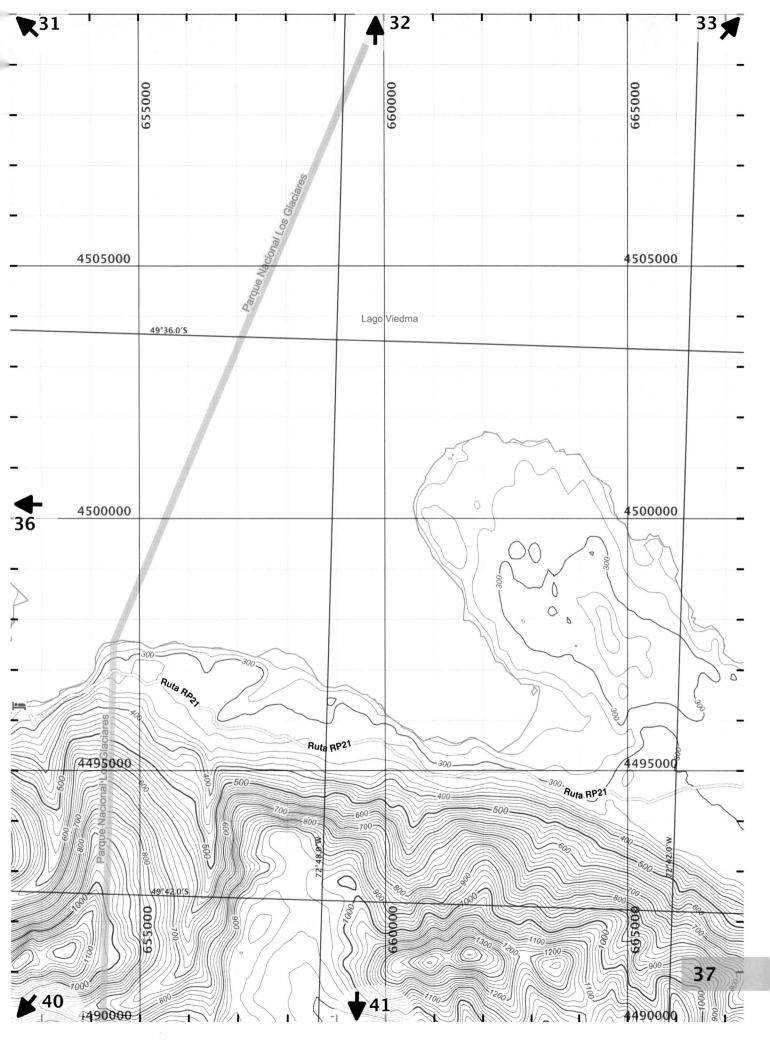

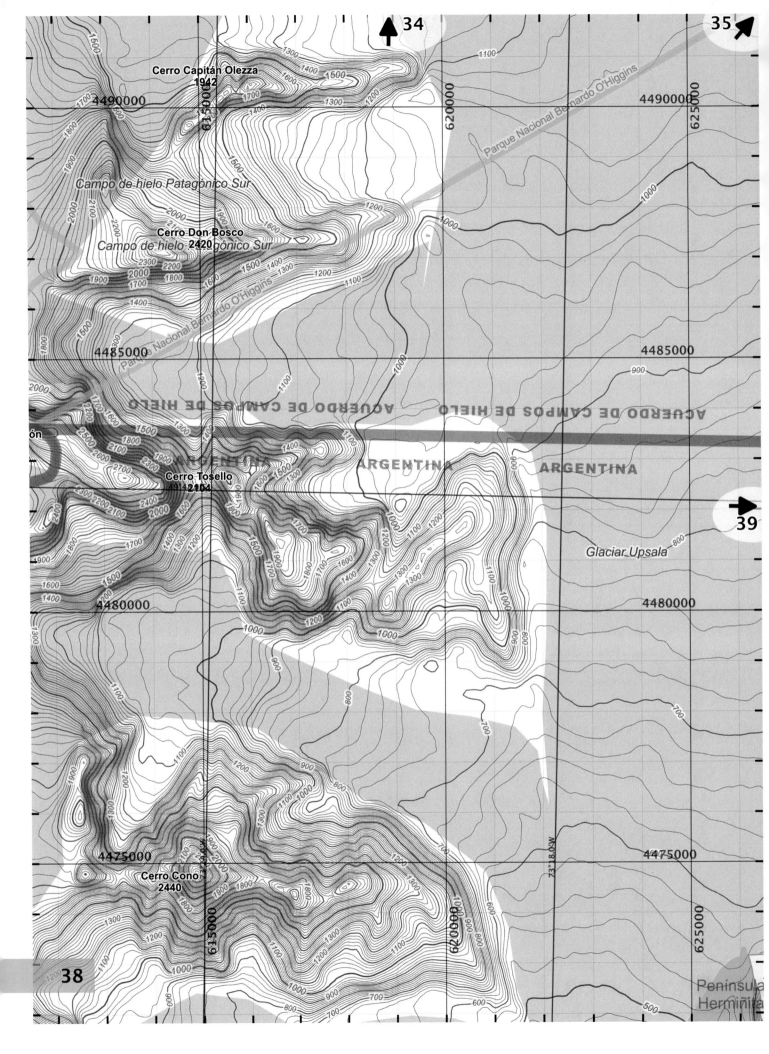

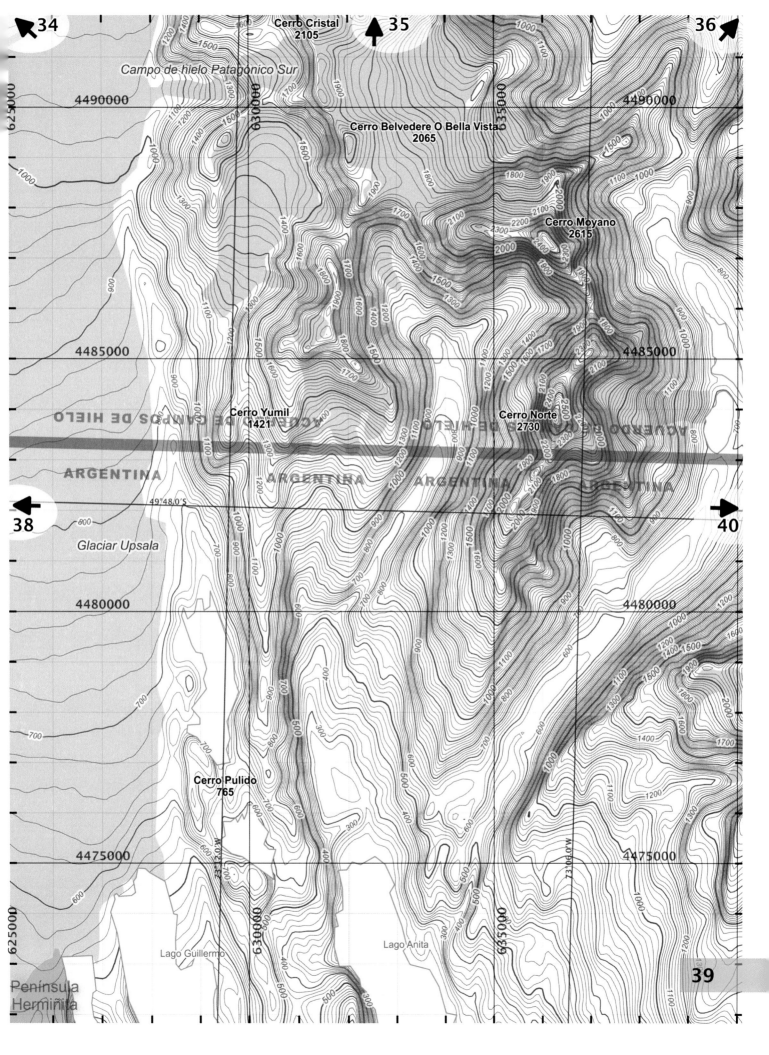

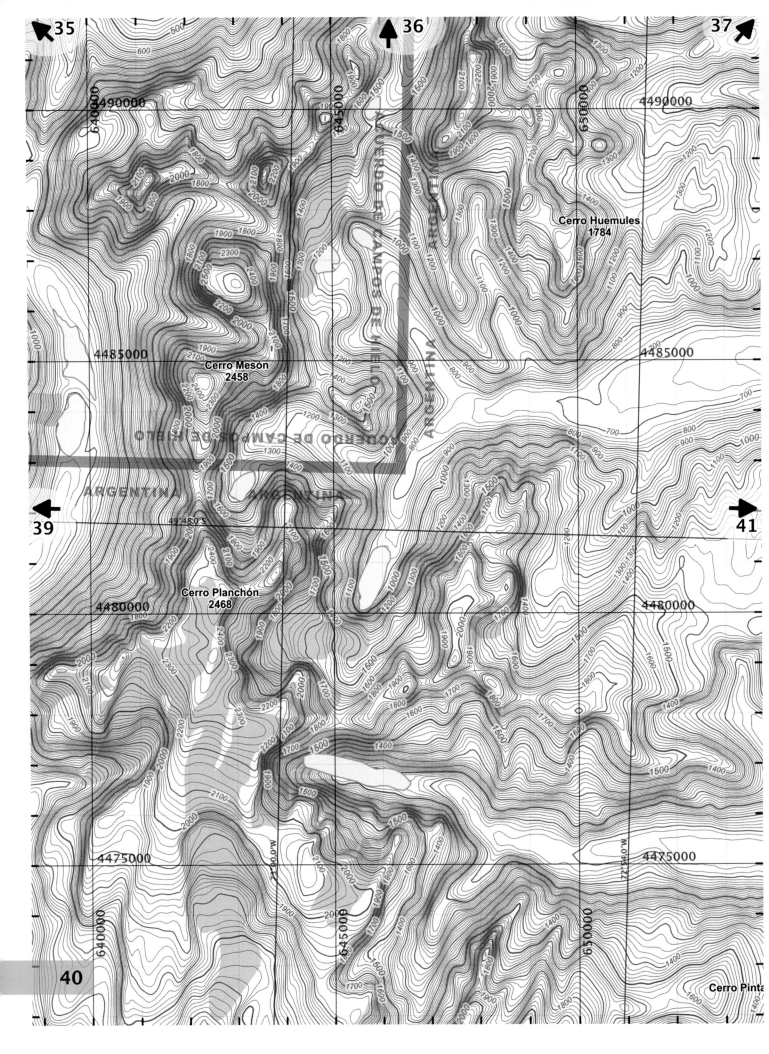

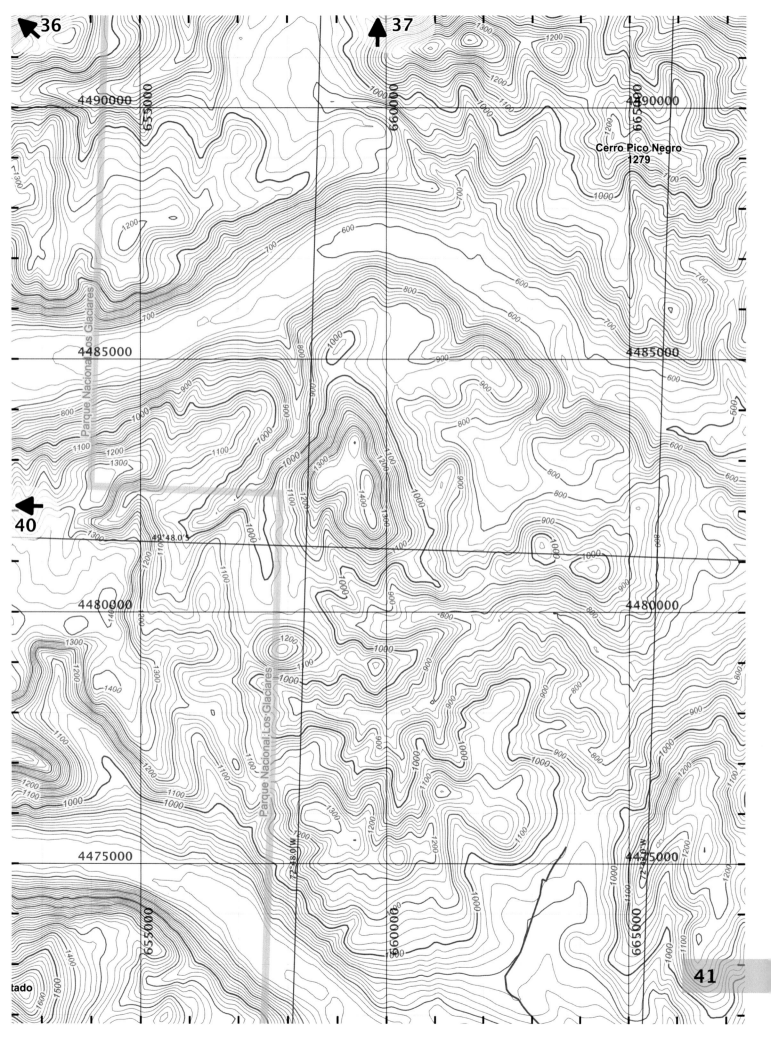

No Warranty: This map is provided to you "as is," and you agree to use it at your own risk. The publisher and its licensors make no guarantees, representations or warranties of any kind, express or implied, arising by law or otherwise, including but not limited to, content, quality, accuracy, completeness, effectiveness, reliability, merchantability, fitness for a particular purpose, usefulness, use or results to be obtained from this map product, This map product is intended to be used only as entertainment and a supplementary travel aid and must not be used for any purpose requiring precise measurement of direction, distance, location or topography. The publisher makes no warranty as to the accuracy or completeness of the map data in this map product.

Map & Atlas Design Copyright © Sergio Mazitto Topo Maps, 2017

Some map data Copyright © Openstreetmap contributors

Published by Sergio Mazitto